4/03

AMERICA AT WAR

WORLD WAR I

Scott Marquette

Rourke Publishing LLC
Vero Beach, Florida 32964

Rourke
Publishing LLC

PHOTO CREDITS: Marine Corps Art Collection: cover, page 7; U.S. Army Center of Military History: pages 20, 40; Defense Visual Information Center: pages 4, 6, 10, 12, 14, 16, 18, 22, 28, 30, 32, 34, 36, 38, 42, 44; National Archives and Records Administration: page 26; Library of Congress: page 24.

PRODUCED by Lownik Communication Services, Inc. www.lcs-impact.com
DESIGNED by Cunningham Design

Library of Congress Cataloging-in-Publication Data

Marquette, Scott.
   World War I / Scott Marquette.
      p. cm. – (America at war)
   Includes bibliographical references and index.
   ISBN 1-58952-392-X
   1. World War, 1914-1918–Juvenile literature. 2. World War,
1914-1918–United States–Juvenile literature. I. Title: World War 1.
II. Title: World War One. III. Title. IV. Series.

D522.7 .M27 2002
940.3–dc21   2002001237

Printed in the USA

Cover Image:
U.S. Marines break through German defenses on the last night of World War I, November 10, 1918.

Table of Contents

World War I was the first war that was fought all over the Earth. More than 30 million men died or were wounded in the war.

Introduction

The War to End All Wars?

As the world entered the second decade of the 20th century, it had seen many wars. But it was about to see something new. It was a war that would engulf the whole Earth. People called it "The Great War." Today, we call it World War I.

The war involved 32 countries, from every part of the world. It was the first **total war**. That meant it involved more than just soldiers. The countries that fought called on all their people to help the war effort.

World War I also saw new heights of killing. Terrible new weapons made war more deadly than ever. About half of the 65 million men who fought were killed or wounded.

People hoped that if the U.S. and its allies won the war, it would lead to a lasting peace. They called it "The War to End All Wars." But World War I did not bring peace. Instead, it sowed the seeds of an even bigger, deadlier war to come.

Most of the war was fought in deep
trenches like this one.

Europe, 1914-1918

Central Powers

The Allies

Neutral

WORLD WAR I TIMELINE

1914

June 24: Archduke Ferdinand is killed

June 28: Austria-Hungary declares war on Serbia

August 1: Germany declares war on Russia

August 4: Germany invades Belgium; England declares war on Germany

September 6: French and British troops hold off Germans at First Battle of the Marne

November: Fighting bogs down at the Western Front

1915

May 7: Germans sink the British ship *Lusitania* killing 128 Americans

1917

April 6: Congress votes to enter the war on the Allied side

December: Bolsheviks take power in Russian Revolution

1918

January 8: President Wilson announces 14-point peace plan

March 3: Russia pulls out of the war

July 15: Allied troops defeat Germans at the Second Battle of the Marne

September 12: U.S. troops win Battle of Saint-Mihiel

September 26: Allied troops begin the Battle of the Argonne

November 9: German government falls

November 11: Allies and Germany sign the armistice, ending the war

A Powder Keg Explodes

By 1914, Europe was a tense place. Strong countries had formed two **alliances**. Germany, Italy, and Austria-Hungary said they would help each other fight if war should come. In reply, England, France, and Russia made a pact to defend each other.

The two sides did not trust each other. Each thought the other would be the first to start a war. The two alliances started an **arms race**. They built guns and ships and raised huge armies. The more the two sides prepared for war, the more afraid they became. Europe was like a keg of gunpowder ready to explode.

Then on June 18 a match was lit. The Archduke Ferdinand, who was to be king of Austria-Hungary, was shot to death. His killer was a man from Serbia. Austria-Hungary said that Serbia had planned the murder. It wanted to strike back. Austria-Hungary declared war on Serbia on July 28.

Events soon spun out of control. Russia got its army ready for war. Alarmed, Germany declared war on Russia. Then, in August, Germany

Soon after the start of the war, both sides were dug in along the Western Front. Neither side could move ahead.

10

marched into France and Belgium. Germany hoped to strike a blow that would end the war. But the French army fought fiercely and held on until British troops arrived to help.

England, France, and Russia were called the **Allies**. Italy dropped out of its pact with Germany and joined the Allies. Germany and the countries that helped it were known as the **Central Powers**. By the end of the year, both sides had dug in along a line near **Ypres**, Belgium. Neither force could move ahead. They would hold these same positions for three bloody years. The area of fighting would be known as the **Western Front**. The Central Powers were also fighting Russia on the Eastern Front near Poland.

In the U.S., President Woodrow Wilson tried to stay out of the war. People felt that Americans should not fight a war across the

Kaiser Wilhelm II

Wilhelm II was Kaiser, or King, of Germany during World War I. He wanted Germany to be a major power in the world. He pushed his country into war. But after the war started, he could not control his government. He had to give up the throne in 1918.

Kaiser Wilhelm II (right) thought the war
would be a chance to make Germany
a major power in the world.

sea. Wilson won the vote in 1916 because he said he would keep the U.S. at peace.

But America helped the Allies with food and supplies. Germany tried to stop the flow of goods. It used **submarines** to sink Allied ships. On May 7, 1915, the Germans sank the British ship *Lusitania*. Almost 2,000 people died in the attack. More than 120 U.S. citizens were killed.

At last, Wilson had enough. With the Allies getting weaker, and German submarines loose on the seas, he asked Congress to vote for war. On April 6, 1917, the U.S. entered World War I.

After it declared war, the U.S. rushed to train soldiers to fight.

The Slow Crusade

Even though the U.S. officially went to war in 1917, it took more than a year to get more than a few troops to Europe. The country had a small army. It had never fought the kind of war it now faced. The U.S. needed more men to fight, and it had to train those men.

Not enough men would volunteer to fight. Wilson decided to ask for a law that would **draft** men into the armed forces. This meant they would have to fight even if they did not want to. Some people thought the draft was wrong. But in just a few months, more than 10 million men had been drafted for military service.

Once the men were trained, they had to be sent to Europe by ship. Moving that many men took a long time. The ships that took them across were in danger. German submarines would sink them if they could.

The U.S. troops sent to the war were called the American Expeditionary Force. Wilson put General John "Blackjack" Pershing in charge. A few U.S. troops got to Europe as early as June 1917. But there were not many, and they did not see much action that year.

*U.S. troops arrive in Scotland in 1918
on their way to the Western Front.*

While the U.S. moved its troops, the Allies were dealt a major blow. Russia had a **revolution**. The Russian people were angry about the long war. Soldiers on the Eastern Front were freezing and starving. Most were dressed in rags. Life was also getting worse and worse for farmers and workers in Russia.

In 1917, angry soldiers and civilians forced the Russian leader, or **Czar**, to leave his throne. A new group, the **Bolsheviks**, took power. They promised to end the war and turn all power over to the people. They signed a peace treaty with the Central Powers. With Russia out of the war, Germany could send more men to the Western Front.

Germany now thought it had to win the war quickly. It knew it had to win before more U.S. troops came to help the Allies. In March 1918, the Germans stormed the Allied forces in the Somme area of France. They sent three times as many men as the

Trench War

World War I was fought in trenches, which were long, straight ditches dug in the ground. Men hid in the trenches and shot at the enemy. Millions of men died trying to attack the trenches. They were usually killed before they could even get close.

By the time most American troops reached battlefields in France, the war had already dragged on for three long years.

British and French had there. Germany thought it could march all the way to the French capital, Paris.

Allied troops fought desperately to slow the Germans. At first, they lost ground. But the German troops were also tired from long years of war. They could not keep up the advance. The big attack failed to win the war for Germany.

The Battle of the Marne in France was one of the first in which the U.S. troops made a real difference.

Over There

By the summer of 1918, almost half a million U.S. troops had arrived in France. They had little experience of war. But the soldiers were young and strong. They had not suffered from years of hunger and fighting as the Allied troops had. The British soldiers called them **Yanks**. It was time to show what the Yanks could do.

In July, the German army attacked the Allies again, near the Marne River in France. It was the second time they tried to take Paris. But this time, 85,000 U.S. troops—along with French and British soldiers—were there to stop them.

The battle went on for five long days. The loss of life on both sides was very high. About 12,000 U.S. soldiers died in the fight. But they stopped the German advance. It was the last big attack the Germans would make in World War I.

The next month, U.S. forces joined British and French troops in an attack near Albert, France, on the Western Front. They forced the German army to flee and took 8,000 of its men as prisoners. The tide was turning against the Central Powers.

At first, the U.S. forces were commanded by Allied generals. But General Pershing wanted to do

*The airplanes used in World War I were lightweight
and could be shot down easily.*

things his own way. He insisted that he command the U.S. troops as a separate army. In the end, the Allies let Pershing take charge of the U.S. Army.

Now it was the Yanks' turn to attack. In September, General Pershing and 300,000 of his troops advanced on a part of the German line near St.-Mihiel, France. In the air overhead were 1,400 warplanes from the new U.S. Air Service. It was one of the first times America used the airplane as a weapon of war. The Germans tried to pull back, but it was too late. The U.S. troops ran over them and captured the whole area.

The Americans helped the Allies take back more land than the Germans had held. They joined the British for an attack on German troops at Meuse-Argonne in France. Along with planes, the Yanks used another new weapon, **tanks**. These were vehicles protected with

Woodrow Wilson

President Wilson did not look like a man of war. He was the son of a minister and taught at a college before he had run for office. He felt bad about going to war after telling the voters he would keep the peace. But he led the nation to victory.

President Woodrow Wilson promised to keep the U.S. out of European war. But he felt forced to go to war anyway.

heavy plates of steel. The tanks had cannons to fire at the enemy. The tanks could get close to the German trenches.

With more than 300 tanks, Pershing's forces slowly advanced on the German lines. But the German army faced another deadly foe. **Influenza**, a disease that killed many soldiers, swept through the German lines. Badly weakened, the Germans pulled back.

The Battle of the Argonne was a success for the Allies. It was also the beginning of the end for the Central Powers.

Posters like these encouraged Americans at home to give money to support the war effort.

The First "Total War"

World War I was the first total war. It involved everyone who lived in the countries that fought—not just the soldiers. In Europe, total war meant that even civilians could be killed by bombs dropped from planes and balloons. In America, it meant that the war would have a big impact on the daily lives of people.

At first, many Americans did not like the war. Two of the biggest groups of people who had come to live in the U.S. were from Germany and Ireland. People who had come from Germany were proud of the new strength of their old country. They still had families in Germany and were afraid of what a war would do to them. The Irish did not want to support

Wheatless Monday

To save food for the troops, people back home would give up certain foods on certain days. There were wheatless Mondays, meatless Tuesdays, and porkless Wednesdays. Instead, people ate whale, horse, and sugarless candy.

With men away at war, many women took jobs in factories, making weapons and ammunition.

England. They did not like the fact that England had control of Ireland.

But the government worked hard to gain support for the war. It printed posters that called on people to save Europe. Popular songs like "Over There" made people feel patriotic:

"Over there! Over there!
Send the word, send the word, over there!
That the Yanks are coming, the Yanks are coming,
The drums rum-tumming everywhere!"

The U.S. stepped up its war effort. It called on factories to stop making things for use at home. Instead, factories made tanks and bombs. The government asked people to grow more of their own food. Posters asked people to "Eat less wheat, meat, sugar and fats to save for the army and our allies."

The government also had to raise money to build weapons and support the army. It created **Liberty Bonds**, and asked people to buy them to support the war. After a few years, they could turn the bonds in for more money than they had paid for them. Many towns and cities in the U.S. had big Liberty Bond drives.

With millions of men in the armed forces, women

Families were encouraged to grow their own food in "victory gardens" so more food could be sent to soldiers overseas.

were called on to work in the factories. It was dirty, dangerous work. Many women were killed in weapons plants when the bombs they were making blew up. But the work made women feel they were doing something important for their country. It gave them a taste of life outside the home.

By the end of the war, America was feeling strong and proud. People were feeling very patriotic. Everyone had been asked to sacrifice for the war effort, so people at home felt they had played a part in the victory.

A new invention—the tank—let Allied troops get close to enemy trenches.

Armistice

With the losses on the Western Front, morale in Germany was sinking fast. The German people were hungry. They were sad from the loss of so many men. The people became angry. They began to riot in the streets.

The German generals knew it was time to ask for peace. They did not want a revolution in their own country like the one that had happened in Russia. If the war did not end soon, it would be a disaster for Germany.

Early in 1918, the German government asked President Wilson for an **armistice**. An armistice was an agreement to end the war. Wilson gave them his own plan for peace. He called it the **Fourteen Points**. It called for Germany to give up all the land it had taken. It also called for Germany to give up submarine warfare. In return, the country would not be punished too hard for its role in the war.

Many Germans did not like Wilson's plan. They thought the plan would make Germany too weak. But many of the Allies also did not like the Fourteen Points. They wanted to punish Germany. They felt the Germans should be made to pay for

Powerful guns like these could fire
28 rounds of ammunition a minute and
hit targets more than a mile away.

their huge war debts. And the Allies wanted to cripple Germany so it could never make war again.

But even though many people on both sides did not like the plan, they had to go along with it. Germany felt it could not fight any longer. The Allies needed U.S. support. The two sides met in France to work out an armistice.

While they met, the war went on. The Central Powers started to fall. In September, Bulgaria gave up the war. The Ottoman Empire gave up the next month. And Austria-Hungary split apart as its people decided to form three new countries.

Then the German government fell. In November, Kaiser Wilhelm had to leave his throne and go into hiding. The new **socialist** leaders declared that Germany was now a **republic**. They quickly agreed to the Allies' terms for peace.

Killing Machines

One weapon that made World War I so deadly was the machine gun. It was a gun that could fire many bullets in just a few seconds. From a trench, one man with a machine gun could kill hundreds of enemy soldiers as they charged.

The declaration of the armistice caused wild celebrations around the world. Here, thousands gather in Philadelphia before a replica of the Statue of Liberty.

On November 11, the Allies and the Germans signed the armistice. Later that morning, fighting stopped on the Western Front. It was the 11th hour of the 11th day of the 11th month of 1918.

All over the world, people broke into wild celebrations. A war that had dragged on for four long years and had killed more than 10 million men had ended at last.

The fighting in Europe left many cities in ruins.
France was one of the countries hit hardest.

"This Is Not Peace"

The armistice ended the fighting. But it was not a lasting peace agreement. That came when both sides signed the Treaty of Versailles in June of 1919. The treaty made Germany pay a terrible price for its part in the war. Some people thought the treaty was so hard on Germany it could not last. A French general said, "This is not peace. It is an armistice for twenty years."

World War I had a huge impact on the world. It would take Europe many years to recover from the loss of so many men and the destruction of so many towns and cities. New countries came into being. Nations such as Czechoslovakia, Yugoslavia, and Austria were formed from old empires. Other countries had their boundaries redrawn.

Many of the young men who fought in the war thought that there would be a new world when peace came. But the new world was very much like the old one. This made the young people in the 1920s and 1930s question the meaning of freedom and democracy. Some thought these words had no meaning at all.

African-American soldiers who fought in World War I came home expecting new rights and freedoms.

They started to live a wild, carefree life. They were called the Lost Generation.

Even older adults began to think about war differently. In the U.S., more people thought the nation should stay out of all wars. These **isolationists** thought that the country would do better to focus on things at home.

Women came back with new hopes from the factories where they had worked. They felt more independent. They thought they should have new rights like the right to vote. In the U.S., women got the right to vote in 1920. African Americans who fought in the war also came back with new hopes. They wanted more of the freedoms for which they had fought. They began to organize to gain their rights.

People hoped that

John "Blackjack" Pershing

Like President Wilson, General Pershing started life as a teacher. But he joined the army in the 1880s and became an officer. He began his war career fighting the Sioux and Apache tribes in the American West.

General "Blackjack" Pershing led
U.S. troops in World War I.

World War I would be the war to end all wars. But other changes from the war would lead to new wars. Russia adopted a **communist** form of government. Its leaders thought they should make all economic decisions for the good of the people and not leave them up to private business.

Even though Russia would be a U.S. ally in the next war, the two countries would come into conflict in later years. The U.S. would try to stop the spread of communism to other countries.

Germany suffered greatly after the war. There were few jobs, and very little food. The government had almost no money because it had to pay its war debt. People became desperate. They looked for a strong new leader. That leader was Adolf Hitler. And in the 1930s, just 20 years after World War I, Hitler would lead the Germans into another terrible world war.

*World War I was not the "war to end all wars."
This World War I veteran holds the flag that covered the
casket of his son who was killed in the Korean War.*

Further Reading

Gurney, Gene. *Flying Aces of World War One*. Random House, 1965.

Hoobler, Dorothy. *Florence Robinson: The Story of a World War I Girl*. Silver Burdett, 1997.

Kudlinski, Kathleen V. *Hero Over Here: A Story of World War I*. Viking, 1991.

Ross, Stewart. *Assassination in Sarajevo: Trigger for World War I*. Heinemann, 2001.

Zeinert, Karen. *Those Extraordinary Women of World War I*. Millbrook, 2001

Websites
The Great War www.pbs.org/greatwar/

World War I: Trenches on the Web www.worldwar1.com

Encyclopaedia of the First World War
www.spartacus.schoolnet.co.uk/FWW.htm

Sow the Seeds of Victory! Posters from the Food Administration During World War I
www.nara.gov/education/cc/foodww1.html

Glossary

alliances — agreements between countries to help each other

Allies — the countries that fought on the U.S. side in World War I; they included England, France, Russia, and Italy

armistice — a temporary agreement to stop fighting

arms race — when two or more countries compete to build up their armies and weapons

Bolsheviks — the socialist party that took control during the Russian Revolution

Central Powers — the countries that fought on the German side in World War I; they included Austria-Hungary, the Ottoman Empire, and Bulgaria

communist — a party that believes that government should make all economic decisions on behalf of the people

Czar — the leader of Russia before the revolution

draft — to force people to serve in the armed forces by law

Fourteen Points — President Wilson's plan for peace in Europe

influenza — a highly contagious disease

isolationists — people who believe that their country should not get involved in other countries' affairs

Liberty Bonds — papers sold during World War I to raise money for the war effort

republic — a government not run by a king

revolution — a sudden change in government, usually by an uprising of the people

socialist — a party that believes that workers should control all factories and businesses

submarines — ships that travel under the water

tanks — steel-plated vehicles with guns

total war — a war that involves all the people of a country

trenches — long, straight ditches in the ground

Western Front — the area of France and Belgium where Allied and Central Powers troops faced each other for most of World War I

Yanks — a name for U.S. soldiers

Ypres — the town of southwestern Belgium near the site of the Western Front

Index